Grandpa

Alison Hawes
Illustrated by Liz Catchpole

Rigby®
A Harcourt Achieve Imprint

www.Rigby.com

Grandpa and Skip went to the fair.

3

"Can you help me get up?"
said Skip.
"Yes," said Grandpa.

4

"Thank you," said Skip.

Skip put his coat down.

"Can you help me get in?"
said Skip.
"Yes," said Grandpa.

"Thank you," said Skip.

Skip got a bear.
He put his bear down.

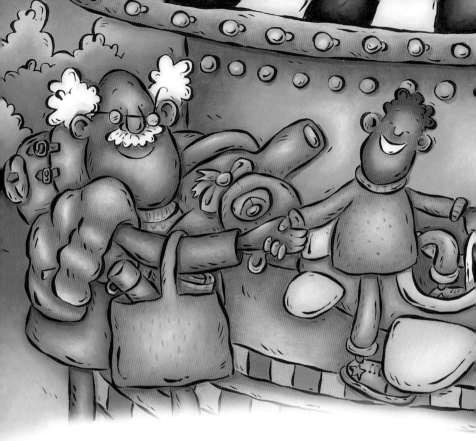

"Can you help me get on?" said Skip.

"Yes," said Grandpa.

"Thank you," said Skip.

"Can you help **me** get up?"
said Grandpa.
"Yes," said Skip.

"Thank you," said Grandpa.